The Jung Frogs

Story by Jenny Giles
Illustrations by Jenny Mountstephen

One day, two frogs
jumped down from a tree.
Mother Frog said,
"I want to lay my eggs
in the river.
But I can't find a safe place.
I don't want the fish
to eat my eggs."

Father Frog said,
"I will make a safe place
for your eggs here by the river.
I can make a little pool
with a wall of mud around it.
Then you can lay your eggs
in the pool."

Father Frog got some mud,
and he made a wall with it.

Father Frog put a lot of mud
on the wall.
He went round and round and round.

He worked for a long time.
The wall got bigger and bigger.

Mother Frog said,
"I like this pool.
I like this big wall, too.
The fish can't swim over it.
They can't get into the little pool.
Now I can lay my eggs."

Father Frog said,
"The little tadpoles
can come out of the eggs
and swim in the pool.
They will be safe, too."

"You have made a very good place for me to lay my eggs," said Mother Frog.
"And it will be a very good home for the little tadpoles."

"Thank you, Father Frog.
You are **so** clever."